A Book of
GREEK COINS

———

Gold and silver coined money
was an invention of the Greeks,
and the text of this little book
provides a scholarly as well as
eminently reliable survey of
Greek coinage from its beginning
to the time of Alexander the
Great. It is a condensed survey;
yet many important historical
issues and masterpieces of en-
graving are mentioned.

Dr Charles Seltman, Fellow
of Queens' College, Cambridge,
has devoted a lifetime to the
study of the subject and has
written scientific books on nu-
mismatics, a general history of
Greek coinage, and publications
on the artistic merit of these
miniature works of art. Many
coins on the plates are shown enlarged in order that the full fineness of detail may be appreciated.

THE KING PENGUIN BOOKS

63

A BOOK OF GREEK COINS

A BOOK OF GREEK COINS

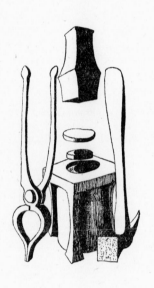

BY CHARLES SELTMAN

PENGUIN BOOKS · LONDON

THE KING PENGUIN BOOKS

EDITOR: N. B. L. PEVSNER · TECHNICAL EDITOR: R. B. FISHENDEN
PUBLISHED BY PENGUIN BOOKS LTD, HARMONDSWORTH
MIDDLESEX, ENGLAND
PENGUIN BOOKS INC, 3300 CLIPPER MILL ROAD, BALTIMORE
MARYLAND, U.S.A.
PENGUIN BOOKS PTY LTD, 200 NORMANBY ROAD
MELBOURNE, AUSTRALIA

THIS BOOK
FIRST PUBLISHED
1952

TEXT PAGES PRINTED BY ROBERT CUNNINGHAM AND SONS LTD, ALVA
PHOTOGRAVURE PLATES MADE AND PRINTED BY
HARRISON AND SONS LTD, LONDON
COVER DESIGN AND MAP BY WILLIAM GRIMMOND
TITLE-PAGE VIGNETTE BY THOMAS MORRIS
MADE IN GREAT BRITAIN

I

PLANTS, birds, beasts and heraldic symbols, portraits
and personifications are present upon the coins in our
pockets and hand-bags to-day because the Greeks first
thought of such things. Although this book is *A Book of Greek
Coins*, it is also, by implication, an introduction both to all
coinage as a commercial convenience and to coinage as a means
to the publication of fine art. There is probably no other product of mankind in which two such diverse needs have for so
long found their fulfilment; for the need to satisfy economic
convenience is one thing – the need to indulge artistry is quite
another. Yet, ever since European man began to coin, he has
constantly – within his Age and his changing ephemeral tradi-
tions – tried to make his money simultaneously useful and attractive. On the whole it is surprising to find how often he has
succeeded in this aim, and how great is the number of fine and
admirable coins which were made between the seventh century B.C. and the reign of King Charles II.

It began among the leaders of commerce in western Asia
Minor, where kings of Lydia and merchant princes in Ionian
cities like Miletus used pellets of white gold (1) and found that
the variability in the gold and silver content of such lumps
called for some form of guarantee. And so they set the seal of
the State upon these pellets. Half a lion (2, 7) was the badge
of the Lydian kings, and heraldic animals (3, 4, 5) emblazoned
the early Ionian coins. By 600 B.C. King Alyattes set, in Lydian
script, part of his name, 'Walwesh(attes)', in front of his lion
(7); and fifty years later, his famous successor, the millionaire
Croesus, stopped minting indeterminable white gold and introduced the earliest pure gold coinage (8) in history. With this
went an issue of pure silver, and the money of the last and
most famous of Lydian kings served as a pattern for the suc-
ceeding coinage of the kings of Persia. Here, upon the golden

Daric and silver shekel (9, 10) of the empire of the Medes and Persians, there appeared a picture of the Great King robed and crowned. Meanwhile, in numerous Greek colonies of Ionian origin, like Hyele (6) in south Italy, and Cyzicus (11, 12) on the shores of the Marmara Sea, admirable coins made after the old Ionian fashion were regularly produced.

Not very long after the easterly Greek merchants started to make coins, the men of old Greece followed suit. As they had no local gold they minted from the beginning in silver; and the tradition that this began under the patronage of Pheidon king of Argos and in the mercantile State of Aegina about 660 B.C., is supported by material evidence. A series of well-made denominations, all stamped with Aegina's blazon, a turtle (13, 14, 15), represents the earliest of all issues in old Greece. Neighbour-states one by one – Argos (16), Paros (17), Corinth (18, 19) and Athens (20) – took up the new convenient aid to commerce, and each one of them decorated its coinage with a blazon appropriate to the State.

Much of the export trade of Athens even before 600 B.C. consisted of fine painted vases, a fact which may explain the first amphora, or wine-jar, on the city's first coins (20); and when the famous legislator Solon adopted a different weight-standard for the State's money, the vase still remained the blazon (21). But when he withdrew from affairs, certain oligarchic politicians who came into power began to mint with their own family coats-of-arms – such as a wheel, horse, bull's head or horse's hindquarters (22, 23, 24, 25) – upon the coinage. An abrupt end was set to this procedure, as will shortly appear.

Meanwhile northern Greeks, and neighbours who along the north shores of the Aegean sea came under Greek influence, were awakened to the advantages of silver money and began to coin. Whole human figures and big powerful animals early became favoured coin-types in Macedonia and Thrace. It was a frontier region where men and women were tough and in which the pictured encounters of satyrs and nymphs (26, 28, 30) reflected the untroubled loves of farmers and vintagers and

6

their girls. Big muscular men herded the cattle (29) or drove oxen harnessed to massive creaking carts (31); while the cattle themselves often fell victims to lions, then common in south-east Europe. The Greek city of Acanthus in Macedonia took as its coat-of-arms a lion destroying a big bull (27).

Before most of these simple, northern, one-sided coins were minted there had appeared in Athens a great innovation which put an end to the older coinage of that city with its family crests. For one noble, seeking power through popular favour, became Dictator of the Athenian people. This was the cele-brated Peisistratus who in the year 566 B.C. founded the great Panathenaic Festival, and probably at the same time introduced the new coinage of Athens (32). Since astuteness is perfectly compatible with piety, this remarkable man may have had a sincere faith in his patron goddess, Athene, whose head he caused to be placed on the large fat silver coins of his city. The reverse was occupied by the coat-of-arms of Athens, an owl – the 'little owl', still common there – and a twig of olive and part of the city's name.

Here in fact is the earliest coinage in the world with a full type on both sides, and at this point it may be of interest to consider how ancient coins were made. An artist or a craftsman would carve an intaglio design on a thick disk of bronze; this was the *obverse* die which fitted into a pit sunk in the top face of an anvil (see title-page vignette). On the lower end of a square-faced bronze punch the man next carved another intag-lio design; this was the *reverse* die. In a little furnace nearby blank disks of silver, carefully adjusted to the correct weight, were heated to make them adequately malleable, and one by one these silver disks were placed with the aid of a pair of tongs upon the anvil over the sunk obverse die. Down upon each disk came the reverse die on the end of the square-faced punch held in a man's left hand. The hammer in his right hand smote several blows upon the upper end of the punch. The tongs pulled the silver disk away for it was now a finished coin which required only to refrigerate.

The men who carved the dies for Greek coins were men of

A MAP OF
ANCIENT GREECE
and the neighbouring countries

MASSALIA

NEAPOLIS

METAPONTUM

TARAS

POSEIDONIA

HERAKLEIA

HYELE

SYBARIS

THURII

CROTON

TERINA

CAULONIA

HIMERA

AETNA

SELINUS

AETNA

ZANKLE

NAXOS

AKRAGAS

CATANA

GELA

SYRACUSE

M E D I T E R

PANTICAPÆUM

BLACK SEA

SINOPE   TRAPEZUS

LETE   ÆNUS

CANTHUS   THASOS   CYZICUS

YNTHUS

MENDE   LYDIA

RACIA   PEPARETHOS   PHOCÆA

DELPHI   CLAZOMENÆ

CORINTH   ATHENS

PHENEUS   ÆGINA   SAMOS   MILETUS

PIA   ARGOS   TROIZEN   CNIDUS   LYCIA

PAROS   RHODES

CYDONIA

SYBRITA

ANEAN   SEA

CYRENE

ALEXANDRIA

varying talents; some were artists of genius, some were good craftsmen doing their best to emulate their gifted exemplars, others – summoned to work in the mint when an emergency called for much coinage – were uninspired smiths incapable of elegant work. Yet it must awake our admiration that during at least four centuries so many coins of perfection, or near perfection, were made by the Greeks.

In Athens the demand for money was so great that many second- and third-rate pieces were produced. Few were as good as the early coin (32) of the reign of Peisistratus, though under his son and successor, Hippias, some masterpieces of art were also made (33). The chubby smiling goddess in the neat helmet, and the well-groomed cocksure owl have a quality that is not surpassed in any other art; in sculpture, painting or the chasing of metals. The earlier of these two is a typical product of Athenian art; the later, of Ionian art made perhaps by an immigrant engraver from Greek Asia Minor. It was such another who made enchanting dies for Peparethus about 500 B.C. The wine-trade of this little island off the coast of Thessaly brought wealth, some of which was turned into coins (34). The large bunch of grapes on the obverse alludes to this trade; but on the reverse the Ionian engraver's free fancy made him set a young winged god speeding madly through the air, his hands grasping wreaths meant for victors: but we cannot tell whether they are for victors in Love or in the Games – whether the young god is Eros or Agōn. Perhaps rich Peparethian wine-merchants knew more about the former.

One early piece struck in a Greek colony – Hyele (6) in Italy – has already been noted; an item in isolation. A more important issue by far was brought forth in curious circumstances by a group of influential states in Greek South Italy. Mnesarchos, an engraver of stones living in Samos, had a famous son, Pythagoras. The latter, versed in metal work, mathematics and music, a profound thinker, migrated about 535 B.C. to South Italian Croton, where he made the coinage, introduced a philosophy, and founded Pythagorean Brotherhoods which presently obtained political control in several prosperous cities;

and in some of these there appeared a coinage in character like that of Croton, but different in appearance from any other Greek money. Each piece displayed in relief the State's blazon and some letters of its name all within a round cable-border, and each piece had on its reverse side the identical picture, but sunk in intaglio. The most famous of these, besides Croton (35) with an Apolline tripod, were Sybaris (36) with a bull looking back, Metapontum (37) with a big ear of barley, Caulonia (38) with an Apollo-statue, Tarentum (39) with a dolphin-rider and Poseidonia (40) with a picture of the statue of its patron-god Poseidon. All these seem to have been made in the three decades before 510 B.C.

Much about the same time certain flourishing Greek cities in Sicily began to issue coins which bore, as was now customary, a civic coat-of-arms; and here one observes that Sicilians had some inclination for punning – or more correctly for 'canting' types. There was a small city called Zankle – later to be renamed Messana – which pictured a dolphin inside a big sickle-shaped harbour (43) shown in bird's-eye view. Now in the language of the indigenous Sicilian population the word 'zankle' or 'dankle' mean's a harvester's sickle. So sickle-shaped harbour on coin is symbol of Zankle = sickle; and the pun is painfully complicated for us because native Sicilians were Sicels. At Himera in the north of the island it was not so difficult. The cock (41) is coat-of-arms and he, as herald of the day (Greek *Hēmera*), is a nice pun-type for Himera. *Akragas* was a word meaning 'harsh' or 'strong', usable of an eagle; so that bird became the arms of the city of Akragas (44). But since there is nothing more tedious than a set of puns you may turn with relief to look at a most elegant coin made for the city of Naxos under Mount Etna. This was in part a daughter-city of the Aegean island, Naxos, both states being famed for their potent wines. Here (42) on the coin of Sicilian Naxos is a delightful head of Dionysos and, on the reverse, grapes. For some reason, not yet fully explained, a close link existed between the artists of this city and Athenian painters. But the greatest of all Sicilian Greek cities in power and wealth, and therefore in coinage, the money of which began with an individual type later to be copied by many other western Greeks, was Syracuse.

Landed gentry, whose ancestors had left Corinth in days when trouble brewed, were the governing class about 520 B.C. in Syracuse when coinage began. They must have combined an aptitude for trade with a love of horse-flesh, and therefore a four-horse chariot was chosen as the State's first blazon (45). You have to look closely, for at first there seem to be only two horses. Yet each animal has a deliberate double outline; so count them as four. On the reverse a wide quartered punch-mark carries in its centre a tiny simple head; but some years later this has grown to a full-scale reverse type (46), and you see a gracious young deity, four dolphins swimming around her head, and the name 'of the Syracusans' is cut in elegant letters. This is the patron goddess of Syracuse, Artemis Arethusa, whose freshwater spring surrounded by the salt sea is neatly suggested by the young girl's head and the swimming dolphins.

Here, in small compass, forty-six coins have been used in an endeavour to give a glimpse of the commercial and artistic accomplishments of the Greeks during the two centuries before the fearful menace of oriental despotism threatened extinction to all that was of permanent value in the Greek way of life. The eastern terror was held – and driven back. The effect of this on art and commerce will be the next theme of this essay.

II

SOME soldier or politician of the European mainland is reported at some time to have called the English a disgusting nation, ignorant of and impervious to defeat, which perfidiously continued to fight after being beaten. The Great King of Persia and his Satraps about 480 B.C. must have thought the same thing about the Greeks, even if they did not phrase it. For the Persians from 500 B.C. pressed on and on, eating up Ionians and Aeolians, Greeks of Thrace and Greeks of the Islands. In

490 a pleasant city, Eretria, very close to Athens was razed, and the elated Persians landed in Attica to meet their first formidable failure in the west on the plain of Marathon. That surprising Athenian victory gave Athens, Greece and Europe ten years' respite before the great invasion; and the victory caused an alteration in the types of Athenian coins coincident with a period of civic wealth. The helmet of Athene which had been almost plain (32, 33) was now decorated with upright olive-leaves (47a) in memory of the victory. Those who fought at Marathon thought that Athene herself, in the guise of an owl, had appeared; and years later Aristophanes in his comedy *The Wasps* gave the story fresh currency:

> How we drove their ranks before us,
> Ere the close of eventide;
> As we closed an OWL flew o'er us,
> And the GODS were on our side.

On the coin's reverse (47b) is the bird open-winged, just taking off – the owl of Marathon. This great silver piece has the weight of ten drachmas and was minted, probably in 486 B.C., to be paid to some Athenian entitled to his annual bonus of ten drachmas (purchasing power=about £45 to-day) in silver from the state-owned mines. But this same bonus, voluntarily surrendered, was presently diverted to the construction of that fleet which, as the biggest Greek armament, helped to smash the Persian fleet at Salamis.

A race more volatile than the ancient Greeks, a race less convinced of value in moderation and self-control, might have produced a spate of boastful coinage commemorating the defeat of Persia's efficient power. But thanks were first given to the gods; and in the two essentially pan-Hellenic centres – Olympia and Delphi – coins were struck which seemed to make indirect allusion to the events. Some forty years before money with a flying eagle and a flower-like thunderbolt of Zeus (48) had appeared at Olympia for use when the games were taking place; and sometimes a figure of Nike filled the reverse. But after 480 B.C. that goddess became much more frequent (49);

13

though note that she might be thought the giver of victory in either sport or war. Delphi, where in normal times only small change was minted, received rich thank-offerings from all the allied Greeks; and, since it was a custom to convert precious metals into tripods, cups and figures, one may regard certain rare large coins inscribed *Dalphikōn*, 'of the Delphians' as part of this treasure (50). A brilliant celator, or metal-worker, made the dies. On one side is pictured a pair of silver drinking-horns shaped as rams' heads, two tiny dolphins – the blazon of Delphi – above them. For his reverse the artist appears to have fitted into a chuck four of the little punches – each bearing a tiny dolphin and star – which he used like hall-marks in his work, and so to have created a temporary die.

Immediately after the Persians were expelled the artistic and commercial energy of the Athenians found much scope for expansion, and it may be observed driving north, west and east. The first famous king of the house of Macedon, Alexander I, freed from Persian overlordship began to coin about 479 B.C., and his silver (51) decorated with a young man and a horse makes you think of Athenian painting, just as the neat letters of his name on the reverse could be paralleled in Athenian inscriptions.

When you turn west to Syracuse you may discover one of the loveliest coins ever made, and one which beyond doubt commemorates a great victory. The Phoenicians of Carthage in North Africa had knowledge of Persian plans for the enslavement of Greece, so they judged the time opportune for a big invasion of Sicily from which they hoped to drive all Greeks. Their timing was good, but Gelon, Lord of Syracuse, and Theron, Lord of Akragas and Himera, combined to inflict a terrible defeat on the African armament just as the Greeks were smashing the Persians. It happened that a brilliant Engraver, whose name began with 'Ar . . . ', had recently come to Sicily. This artist, whose manner recalls that of a fine Athenian painter known as Epiktetos II, was commissioned to make dies for a whole series of coins the types of which referred to the victory. Now, Demarete, Queen of Gelon of Syracuse, and sister of the

14

Lord of Akragas, had interested herself in the peace terms imposed on Carthage, and it came to pass that her name was linked with this victory coinage of the year 497 B.C. Upon the obverse (52a) of the big ten-drachma piece is a slow-moving chariot drawn by elegant horses; in the underspace is a panicky lion – African, Carthaginian – in flight. The reverse of the same piece (52b) tantalizes. Who is she? From earlier coins of this State (45, 46) one assumes her to be the city's patron goddess crowned with olive for victory. Her dolphins are there too. The engraver has retained that 'full eye in profile head' convention which Greek art was so reluctant to relinquish because the soul you love or worship seems to be in the eye. But there is a loveliness of an individual creature in this head which tempts you to surmise that the goddess was shown with the features of Demarete, the queen.

Turn east to Asia Minor and its south-western corner where you meet again the influence of Athens, for the efficiency and energy of her sailors increased that State's popularity and opened the way to artists as well as to traders. A man trained in Athenian tradition made some coin-dies for the prosperous ruler of a Lycian city, Antiphellos, where Aphrodite was worshipped. The goddess appears here (54) in the guise of a lady of fashion turned out to perfection. She contrasts with another picture of the same goddess on the coin of another city not far away where, however, Dorian taste prevailed. This was Cnidus in Caria. You can see a coin, made perhaps only five years after the Lycian piece, on which a girlish head of Aphrodite (53) almost Spartan in its simplicity is engraved. The other sides of both these coins have pleasing types the full significance of which escapes us. On the Lycian piece is a patterned symbol of the god Uranus from whom Aphrodite was sprung. On the coin of Cnidus is the forepart of a lion.

Both heads of the goddess still have the full eye, and this same convention is also preserved on another coin, a work perfect in design and restraint made by some Athens-trained artist about 470 B.C. in the northern coastal city of Aenus (55) which lay at the near end of an important trade-route. Hermes as god of commerce was the city's patron and his head in a close-fitting cap is on one side, while the reverse has a powerful he-goat in front of which is the cult-image of the State's god. On a well-made throne stands a primitive idol made from the stem of a conifer on the top of which is a simple carved head, and beside the image is a twisted caduceus, the herald's staff which the god almost always carries.

In relief work as in painting the artists of Greece were slow to abandon their expressive convention of a profile-face with a full eye. They dropped it first for such half-animal creatures as Seilens, the wild horse-tailed followers of Dionysos. So it came about that the earliest coin to show a head with a profile eye is the four-drachma piece of a Sicilian city called Aetna founded near Mount Etna by the Syracusan ruler Hiero. An engraver of unsurpassed ability – whom we know as the Aetna Master – made in 470 B.C. a pair of dies (56): bald, horse-eared, fat, bearded Seilenos is on the obverse; under his neck one of those scarab-beetles which were said to attain unusual size on the volcano's slopes. And, lest such a type should seem over-frivolous for the coin of the realm, the reverse has the compensation of supreme dignity. Here is Zeus himself on a fine throne on the seat of which lies the skin of a wild cat. The god holds a thunderbolt and a long staff. His eagle perches on the swaying tip of a young fir. Hiero's foundation was short-lived, for on his death the original inhabitants, men of Catana, came back in 461 B.C., but they employed the Aetna Master to make them dies for a coin (57) celebrating their return. It shows the god of their favourite river, Amenanos, presented as a swimming man-headed bull. See how his beard matches the beard of Seilenos on the Aetna coin (56). Below a fat fish swims up-stream; above, as it were on the far bank, walks a water-bird. The reverse of the coin has a swiftly-moving Nike. Three versions of this goddess illustrate three variants of Greek art: first the Peloponnesian type in Olympia (49); second this Sicilian figure (57) strongly influenced by the art of Athens; third (80) a goddess of that pan-Hellenic style which owed much to the Master of Olympia himself. From Catana the Aetna Master moved on to a neighbouring city, Naxos, where he made, also probably in 461 B.C., dies for what is perhaps the most splendid of all Greek coins. A Naxian coin with a refined head of Dionysos smiling (42), made thirty years before, has been shown; but when the Aetna Master takes on the carving of a picture of the dread god you cannot fail to be moved (58a). The elegance of beard and lip, the strong neck-muscles, have the same accomplishment as the older coin (56); but while Seilenos has a certain earthy quality, Dionysos has ineffable divinity. On the reverse of the Naxian piece Seilenos, younger, athletically perfect, appears crouching on the ground, facing and turning his head to a wine-cup which he holds (58b). Human animal magnificence is here portrayed as on no other monument.

In the west of Sicily lay a city called Selinus on the banks of a stream of the same name which meant 'celery-river'. About 460 B.C. coins began to appear here with imaginative types. On the larger (59) Artemis drives a chariot and Apollo, standing beside her, is about to shoot, while the reverse shows a youth making a libation between an altar and a base with the little statue of a bull upon it. The youth personifying the river is labelled 'Selinos'. On the lesser coin (60) is Herakles clubbing the Cretan bull, and upon the other side a smaller river god, labelled 'Hypsas', between an altar and a wading-bird. These young demi-gods of the rivers are thought of as making libations to the mightier Olympians. Slow-moving chariots had early been the fashion at Syracuse (45, 46), attaining a new dignity with the Demarete coins (52) and tempting other cities to copy. One example is a fine piece of Catana (61) remarkable for a noble head of Apollo; another is a coin of Gela (62), the chariot driven by Nike, and the reverse showing a head of the local river-god, Gelas. A tiny horn over his forehead is the sole sign of his animal or demi-god nature; otherwise he is a thoughtful well-bred youth. The three fish round his head, one turning, one level, one belly-upwards, are of outstanding excellence, and the whole makes a brilliant design.

Turn for a while from Sicily to consider the coinage of the Greek mainland. Here for the fifty years between the Persian and Peloponnesian wars, Athens was dominant alike in politics, in economics and in art. A democracy, advanced for that age, combined with home silver-mines in the Laureotic region to produce a spate of varied coinage. An Athenian of that day might carry in his bag a ten-drachma and a two-drachma piece (64, 63), though both had actually been minted before the Persian invasion. His common coins were the following: four drachmas (65); one drachma (66)=six obols; half a drachma (67)=three obols; two obols (68); one-and-a-half obols (69); one obol (70); half-an-obol (71); and a tiny silver quarter-obol (72) known as a 'tetartemorion'. All showed a head of the city's Patron, Athene; all but the last had owls on them; the last being too small for an owl, had a mere twig of olive. The mixed sizes of these owls and their varied attitudes are attractive, especially when you consider that the Little Owl lays eggs over a fair period and 'staggers' the hatching, so that a nestful of these birds contains owl-chicks of various ages and sizes. This gives point to a neat passage in *The Birds* of Aristophanes. Promises of prosperity are made to the Athenians in the words:

> Little Laureotic owlets
> Shall be always flocking in:
> You shall find them all about you,
> As the dainty brood increases,
> Building nests within your purses;
> Hatching little silver pieces.

The Athenians, in fact, were fond of their coins, for in money matters familiarity breeds affection for your own and contempt for other peoples' currency. Englishmen and Americans know perfectly well that the beautiful notes issued by the *Banque de France* are works of art, while paper with the signature of Mr Beale and U.S. 'Greenbacks' are quite without artistic merit. Yet we change back to our own currency with a sense of relief, which must have been felt in just the same fashion by an Athenian who changed the lovely money of the Western Greeks for his own rough 'owls'. 'Best of all coins', Aristophanes called the silver of his city.

The appearance of Athene on all these coins had propaganda value for Athens. It will not escape our notice that in an age without newsprint the only 'printed', that is stamped objects with a wide circulation were coins, and these carried ideas to remote lands. The effect may be observed in the West, for Athens began after 445 B.C. to exercise a growing influence upon the Greeks of Italy; first by the foundation of New Sybaris (73) and, when that failed, by establishing Thurii (74, 79), both of which cities took Athene for their Patron. From this centre her influence passed to other Italiote states like Neapolis (75), Herakleia (76, 78) and Hyele (77). On none of these coins is the old-fashioned full-eyed type retained; she is modernised; but all the coins exemplify the fifth-century tradition of Athenian art. A merging of this and Peloponnesian art to form a style which is truly pan-Hellenic can be observed in certain coins minted by states of Peloponnesus. A drachm (81) from the little city of Troizen, ally of Athens though in the land of Argos, has an exquisite head of Athene unhelmeted, the eye still almost full. A trident-head decorates the reverse. The Master of Olympia himself owed a debt to Athenian art, and the influence of his temple-sculptures affected the running Nike (80) on a coin made probably for the Games of 448 B.C. Corinth, while her trade rivalry with Athens grew, came ever more under the spell of Athenian art. This is clear from two coins, one of the mother-city (82), the other of a Corinthian colony called Ambracia (83). The obverses have the State blazon, Pegasus; the reverses a head of Athene, the former (82) resembling a famous marble monument with Athene mourning made in Athens in 458 B.C.

III

IN the history of Greek fifth-century art the event which perhaps had the biggest effect was not the Persian invasion nor the Peloponnesian war, but the outbreak in Athens in 430 B.C. of bubonic plague. It was this horror which drove away so many artists who had found a home there. Potters, builders, carpenters and carvers of stone died, or recovered and remained. Even the work of mason-sculptors in marble was an art subsidiary to the major arts of workers in metal and ivory, of painters and of makers of statues in bronze, and it was those who practised the major arts who sought work elsewhere. Italy and especially Sicily offered them fresh opportunities. This is the explanation of the splendour which shone forth for the next quarter-century in the Greek West. Before this occurred the coins of Syracuse continued in the now normal Sicilian tradition of a slow-moving chariot on one side and a divine head, often of great charm (84, 85) on the other.

The old English word 'celature' (Latin *caelatura*) describes the art of a number of men, almost certainly Athens-trained, who now began to set their signatures upon some of the many Sicilian dies which they made, famous among them being Phrygillos, Euainetos, Herakleidas, Eukleidas and Kimon. A great silver bowl has been found which was certainly made by some member of this group, and its main frieze is a series of four-horse racing chariots exactly like those which now appeared on the coins (86 to 91). Euainetos about 425 B.C. made admirable chariots for Syracuse and Catana; on both a flying Nike carries a tablet with the artist's name (86, 87). The reverses have dainty heads of a young girl and a young boy who represent, one Artemis Arethusa, goddess of Syracuse, the other Catana's river god Amenanos – once bull-shaped (57) – now quite human, a bell on a wool-fillet before his face. Soon after this Catana caused other dies to be made by Herakleidas (88) whose signature runs along the left side of an astonishing frontal head of Apollo. At Syracuse too facing heads became the fashion just after that city had, by the help of her gods, escaped disaster at the hands of the Athenian Expedition and had almost annihilated the invaders. Eukleidas made a clever die (89) with a head of Artemis Arethusa – dolphins in her hair – wearing the triple-crested helmet and Medusa-necklace of her defeated rival, Pallas Athene. The engraver's signature is on the bowl of the helmet under the crests. Such facing heads as these, turned a fraction off absolute frontality, are favoured in the fine art of celature. Of them all, the most sensational and appealing is a work of the famous Kimon (90a) with a facing head of the girl-goddess Arethusa – her name inscribed outside the dotted border, his signature in full on the front of her headband. Dolphins dive in and out of her wind-blown hair, and one comes out over her right shoulder. No finer facing girl's head was ever made, though you will see an Apollo (105) to equal it. To go with this head Kimon made a brilliant chariot-die signing his name between the double lines under the foremost horse's hooves (90b). It is no wonder that tradition preserved for many centuries the name of Kimon as a master of celature.

Almost contemporary with the last piece is a big ten-drachma coin (91a) from the second Sicilian city, Akragas, founded long before by Rhodes whence came the cult of Helios. That god is shown driving his chariot through the noon-day sky; an eagle holding a snake flies upwards, a crab tumbles down to the sea. On the reverse (91b) a splendid pair of eagles recall lines in the *Agamemnon* of Aeschylus telling of an omen seen by the Greeks – two eagles tearing a pregnant hare.

Coins made by engravers, Athenian in tradition, in Greek Italy have been shown (73 to 77), and they were many. There is something idyllic about a coin of Croton (93) with young Herakles seated upon a rock on one side, and on the other a boyish Apollo dodging behind a big tripod to shoot the monstrous Python. Phrygillos, who worked for Syracuse and several other cities, made lovely dies for Terina (92). Here is the head and the whole figure of Nike. She sits on an overturned wine-jar and plays with a bird perched on her finger. At Metapontum there is still the old original blazon (37) of a barley-ear; but it is now on the reverse only, while the obverse (94) shows the head of a young goddess.

The great engraver, Euainetos, continued active in Syracuse, where he appears to have worked from about 425 to 393 B.C. He was the main creator of big silver ten-drachma coins first struck in 412 B.C., to celebrate the overthrow of the Athenian Expedition, and continued perhaps for another twenty years.

Here (96*a*, *b*) is a version of Artemis Arethusa and a racing chariot both of which attained a celebrity in the ancient world which they have regained in our own day. An aggressive war of Carthage against Sicily called for the minting of gold reserves in Syracuse for which Euainetos made dies. The patron goddess is on one side (95); on the other Herakles strangling a lion is a symbol of the Greek hope that Carthage may be made impotent.

At this point you may look for a moment to see what, meanwhile, had been happening in mainland Greece before considering a shift of emphasis which began about 400 B.C. Seventy years before the influence of Athenian art on the northern coast of the Aegean had appeared in the coinage of Aenus (55), and that same influence did not wane. In the rich wine-growing city of Mende in Macedon a single engraver with Athenian tradition made about 430 B.C. a few admirable dies (98) depicting Dionysos, wine-cup in hand, on the back of a plump ass, and, on the other side, a little grape-vine surrounded by the city's name. Failure in the attempts made by certain local 'roughs' to imitate this merely throw into relief the excellence of the artist's work. The strength of an artistic tradition is well exemplified in Peloponnese, where the work of the Master of Olympia still dominated the conceptions of artists who made coins for the Festivals. In 420 B.C., when peace prevailed and great numbers attended the Games, dies were made by a man, who sometimes signed with two letters, Da . . . , and one bore a head of Zeus (97) of great nobility indebted to the temple sculptures' inspiration.

Gifted artists stand little chance of earning a livelihood when great disasters threaten. Such was the Carthaginian invasion of Sicily, which between 409 and 396 B.C. destroyed or enslaved all the great cities in the island, save only Syracuse. Some of the men who made fine dies crossed the straits to Italy; others travelled to the Greek mainland after the Peloponnesian war had ended in 404 B.C. And so you suddenly meet certain coins of exceptional fineness in a number of widely-scattered states.

Three cities in the island of Rhodes, abandoning their ancient sites, combined in 408 B.C. to found a new city – called Rhodes like the island – and chose Helios, the Sun-god, as their divine Patron. The first coins of this new foundation (99) bore on the obverse his facing head, and you may seek far to discover a better impression of the heat in Mediterranean sunshine. On the reverse is a 'still life'; rose and drooping bud and little toy Sphinx. There were links between Rhodes and African Cyrene (100), and again about 400 B.C. the facing head appears. Celature and die-cutting both welcome the chance to produce this kind of tour-de-force. Ammon, the ram-horned bearded god of Libya, akin to the Greek Zeus, is on one side; and on the other, a stem of silphium, used as a drug and a seasoning, the main source of Cyrene's wealth.

By 400 B.C. all Greece was employing an art which it is convenient to term pan-Hellenic, and good examples are to be found in Peloponnese and Crete. A north Arcadian city, Pheneus, lay close by Mount Kyllene, where legend said Zeus had begotten Hermes on the goddess-nymph Maia. Here about 390 B.C. an engraver who signed Po . . . made dies (103) with a head of Maia and a figure of Hermes carrying a little boy, Arkas, supposed ancestor of the Arcadian race. In western Arcadia in 370 B.C. various townships were joined to make a new city, Megalopolis. An early coin, engraved by a man called Olym . . . , had a head of Zeus (104) and a hard, athletic Pan holding a throwing-stick and seated upon a rock. There is unevenness in the money of Cretan cities. You find the work of first-rate men who did not sign, of second-rate men who did, and of engravers with the delicacy of a shoeing-smith who turned out work in emergencies. Two coins by first-rate men will suffice. The first (102) of Cydonia has a vine-crowned girl's head, probably Akakallis daughter of Minos, mother by Apollo of the child Kydon nursed by a bitch. The second coin is of Sybrita (101) and shows – rare phenomenon – a head on either side; Dionysos bearded, a grape-bunch before him, and Hermes, his hat tipped forward to shade his eyes and his caduceus in front. This coin of about 360 B.C. is a masterpiece.

It is now that you may observe one of the most impressive of all coins, a four-drachma-piece with the words 'Theodotos made it', engraved for the Ionian city of Clazomenae (105a). This facing Apollo is a fit companion to the lovely girl Arethusa (90a). There is nothing of the effeminate look which later the god was to assume, but a square jaw, firm chin and well-marked brows. The reverse is a perfect foil to the head: a swan, bird of Apollo and blazon of the city walks, wings up, bold and wild (105b). Around is the name of the state and of a magistrate. Theodotos of Clazomenae was a very great engraver.

Insatiable curiosity took the Greeks far afield, and long ago they had founded colonies in the Crimea, where Scythian chiefs learnt to admire Greek art and coins appeared. In Panticapaeum the biggest city, gold (107) was minted about 380 B.C. with the facing head of Seilenos, shaggy, snub-nosed like Scyths represented on Greek silver vases from the same region. On the reverse is a lion-griffin, guardian of gold-mines, with a spear in his jaws. Here is contrast with a sensitive young Apollo (106) of about 360 B.C. from Chalcidian Olynthus which Philip of Macedon destroyed in 348 B.C. The god's eight-stringed lyre is on the reverse. At Olympia about this time there was set up a statue by the famous Athenian Praxiteles, the celebrated Hermes. Some associate probably made an Olympian coin (108) in 340 B.C. with a gentle pensive head of Zeus and an eagle atop of an Ionic capital.

The gods of Greece might seem to grow more kindly as the King of Macedon grew more ruthless, even though he posed as champion of Pythian Apollo that he might get control of Delphi. Here the Amphictyonic Council issued perhaps at his behest in 335 B.C. some handsome pieces (109) with the head of Demeter corn-wreathed, and with Apollo, long-robed seated on the navel of Earth resting an elbow on his lyre. He seems to look with foreboding into the future as though he could not yet see that the son of Philip was to spread Hellenism through the world.

Sit back, before you consider what Alexander did, to review the wide range of Greek civilization east and west as shown in the coinage. What came from Panticapaeum (107) you have seen; but there were other rich cities in the Black Sea region, like Trapezus (113) which carries a god's head and a table – a punning type this – laden with grapes; or Sinope (114) with a girl's head, Sicilian in style, and a sea-eagle on a dolphin; or Cyzicus with its heavy coinage of white gold (115) and varied types. In the west, Italian Tarentum, grown very rich, issued countless coins (112) with a hero riding a dolphin on one side, and a horseman on the other. One of the latest facing heads, echoing Sicilian art, comes from Metapontum (111) and shows a dainty goddess. Meanwhile, far to the west, Marseilles grew prosperous and struck money with the head of Artemis (110) copied from coins by Euainetos and, on the reverse, a creature more like a poodle than a lion.

IV

THE Greeks had no banks. State funds, and sometimes private savings could be lodged in temples. But if a city was sacked temples were looted. So when father had something to put by he hid it underground and did not always trust his sons enough to tell them where. Countless hoards were never found till modern times: countless hoards still remain to be found by a peasant's plough or spade. Even so there exist to-day myriads of Greek coins minted before Alexander and many hundreds of thousands made after he began to change the world.

In this brief review there are certain gods whose pictures you have often seen; Athene, Apollo and Nike, Zeus and Herakles, the very gods whose images Alexander chose to spread through the world. Apollo's head was on his father's gold the issue of which continued: the other four he took in 336 B.C. as types for the Alexander coinage. On his gold he set Athene's head, copied from a famous bronze statue by Pheidias in Athens, and Nike. On his silver (116) was the greatest of all heroes, Herakles, legendary ancestor of the Macedonian kings; and Zeus Olympios enthroned, Father of gods and men. When, following on his conquests, Alexander opened fresh mints to make these same types in Asia the men of Tarsus took this seated god for their Ba'al, the men of Babylon for Bel-Marduk. In his greatest foundation of all, Alexandria by Egypt, such coins began to appear about 326 B.C. and the finest engraver of Greece was called to make the first dies. Here (116) it is no longer an imaginary Herakles, but the new hero-god, for the face under the lion's scalp is the face of Alexander.

Twenty-three years after his death one of his generals, Lysimachus, set the portrait of Alexander on his coinage (117). There is the upward gaze, the royal diadem and the curving horn of Ammon springing from his brow. It is the noblest portrait head on any Greek coin. On the reverse, another deity, Athene seated. Because men had now less faith in the gods she is not so sure, not so good. But historically she looks back – and forward: back to Alexander's gold, to the bronze statue by Pheidias, to Athene on the money of Athens, and so to Peisistratus: forward to the seated armed goddess *Dea Roma*, to her 'daughter', the figure made on Hadrian's coinage to represent Britannia. This figure was revived under Charles II for our coppers, and is still with us. So you may think of Peisistratus and Pheidias and Alexander when you look at a penny.

SOME BOOKS ON GREEK COINS

ART

Charles Seltman, *Masterpieces of Greek Coinage*, Bruno Cassirer, Oxford, 1949.

G. F. Hill, *Select Greek Coins*, Vanoest, Paris, 1927.

E. Rizzo, *Monete Greche della Sicilia*, Rome, 1946.

A. Gallatin, *Syracusan Decadrachms of the Euainetos Type*, Harvard, 1930.

HISTORY

B. V. Head, *Historia Numorum*, 2nd ed., Oxford, 1911.

G. F. Hill, *Guide to the Principal Coins of the Greeks*, British Museum, London, 1932.

Charles Seltman, *Greek Coins*, Methuen, London, 1933.

LIST OF ILLUSTRATIONS

The following abbreviations are used: E = electrum, i.e. white gold.
G = gold. In the absence of either assume the coin to be silver. c = 'about'.
All dates are B.C. dr = drachm, 2 dr = didrachm, 4 dr = tetradrachm, etc.
st = stater, ob = obol, 2 ob = diobol, 3 ob = triobol, etc. Note that 6 obols
= 1 drachm. *sign* = with signature of artist.

48, 49. OLYMPIA, 2 drs, eagle/bolt and eagle/Nike, c 520 and c 480.

50. DELPHI, 3 dr, rams/dolphins, 479. – **51.** MACEDON, 8 dr, man and horse, c 479.

52. SYRACUSE, 10 dr, chariot/goddess, 479.

53. CNIDUS, dr, lion/Aphrodite, c 470. – **54.** LYCIA, st, Aphrodite/ tetraskeles, c 475.

55. AENUS, 4 dr, Hermes/goat, c 470.

56. AETNA, 4 dr, seilen/Zeus, 470.

57. CATANA, 4 dr, river-bull/Nike, 461.

58. NAXOS, 4 dr, Dionysos/seilen, 461.

59, 60. SELINUS, 4 dr, 2 dr, chariot/river-god and Herakles/river-god, c 465.

61. CATANA, 4 dr, chariot/Apollo, c 450. – **62.** GELA, 4 dr, chariot/ river-god, c 440.

63 to 71. ATHENS, 2 dr, 10 dr, Athene/owl, 486; 4 dr, dr, 3 ob, 2 ob, 1½ ob, ob, ½ ob, Athene/owl. – **72.** ATHENS, ¼ ob, Athene/ twig, All c 460.

73. SYBARIS, 4 ob, Athene/bull, c 445. – **74, 79.** THURII, 2 dr, 4 dr, Athene/bull, c 430 and 410. – **75.** NEAPOLIS, 2 dr, Athene/ bull, c 430. – **76, 78.** HERAKLEIA, 2 drs, Athene/Herakles, c 430 and 410. – **77.** HYELE, 2 dr, Athene/lion on stag, c 420.

80. OLYMPIA, 2 dr, eagle/Nike, 448. – **81.** TROIZEN, dr, Athene/ trident, c 460.

82, 83. CORINTH and AMBRACIA, sts, Pegasus/Athene, c 450 and 440.

84, 85. SYRACUSE, 4 drs, chariot/goddess, c 455 and 445.

86. SYRACUSE, 4 dr, chariot/goddess, c 425. – **87.** CATANA, 4 dr, chariot/river-god, c 425. Both *sign* Euainetos.

88. CATANA, 4 dr, Apollo/chariot, *sign* Herakleidas, c 415.

89. SYRACUSE, 4 dr, chariot/goddess, *sign* Eukleidas, c 412.

90. SYRACUSE, 4 dr, Arethusa/chariot, *sign* Kimon, c 410.

91. AKRAGAS, 10 dr, Helios/eagles, c 411.

92. TERINA, 2 dr, Nike/Nike, *c* 425. – **93.** CROTON, 2 dr, tripod and Apollo/Herakles, *c* 430.

94. METAPONTUM, 2 dr, goddess/barley, *c* 410. – **95.** SYRACUSE, G, 20 dr, goddess/Herakles. *c* 395.

96. SYRACUSE, 10 dr, goddess/chariot, *c* 395.

97. OLYMPIA, 2 dr, Zeus/bolt, *sign* Da . . . . , 420. – **98.** MENDE, 4 dr, Dionysos on ass/vine, *c* 430.

99. RHODES, 4 dr, Helios/rose, *c* 408. – **100.** CYRENE, 4 dr, Zeus-Ammon/plant, *c* 400.

101. SYBRITA, 2 dr, Dionysos/Hermes, *c* 360. – **102.** CYDONIA, 2 dr, Nymph/Bitch and boy, *c* 360.

103. PHENEUS, 2 dr, Maia/Hermes, *sign* Po . . . . , *c* 390. – **104.** MEGALOPOLIS, 2 dr, Zeus/Pan, *sign* Olym . . . . , *c* 370.

105. CLAZOMENAE, 4 dr, Apollo/swan, *sign* Theodotos, *c* 370.

106. OLYNTHUS, 4 dr, Apollo/lyre, *c* 360. – **107.** PANTICAPAEUM G, st, seilen/griffin, *c* 380.

108. OLYMPIA, 2 dr, Zeus/eagle, *c* 340. – **109.** DELPHI, 2 dr, Demeter/Apollo, 335.

110. MASSALIA, dr, Artemis/lion, *c* 350. – **111.** METAPONTUM, G, 4 ob, goddess/barley, *c* 334. – **112.** TARENTUM, 2 dr, Phalanthus/horseman, *c* 344.

113. TRAPEZUS, dr, god/table, *c* 410. – **114.** SINOPE, dr, goddess/sea-eagle, *c* 405. – **115.** CYZICUS, E, st, Hermes and vase.

116. ALEXANDRIA, 4 dr, Alexander as Herakles/Zeus, 326. – **117.** KING LYSIMACHUS, 4 dr, Alexander as a god/Athene, *c* 300.

*

The coins described above are or were preserved in the following collections:

Berlin, 47, 64, 87, 108; Boston, Museum of Fine Arts, 55, 89 (obverse), 109, 115; Brussels, 56, 62; C. Gillet, 97; The Hague, 82, 84, 102; R. C. Lockett, 16, 59, 60, 61, 68, 106, 111, 113, 114; Munich, 91; Bibliothèque Nationale, Paris, 50, 105; Baron Penisi, 88 (obverse), 90, 96 (obverse); Charles Seltman, 7, 10, 13, 14, 15, 65, 67, 69, 70, 71, 72, 81, 116, 117; John Seltman, 6, 17, 53; E. G.

Spencer-Churchill, 32, 95; W. H. Woodward, 104 (reverse). All the rest are in the British Museum.

A few of the photographs are taken from electrotype facsimiles, but the majority direct from the original coins. The author of this book wishes to thank the Heads of Departments, Keepers, and private collectors for their generous co-operation.

Cover. The coins on the outside cover are: top-left, TERINA, silver, Nike, c 425 B.C.; top-right, LYSIMACHUS, silver, Athene, c 300 B.C.; bottom-right, ANTONINUS PIUS, bronze, Roma, A.D. 151; bottom-left, George VI, penny. All four are slightly enlarged.

All coins shown in the plates are actual size except where a size is mentioned in the caption. Where a size is given it is that of the original diameter. Thus on plate 8, '1.4 in.' means that the diameter of the original coin is 1.4 inches. *c* means *circa*.

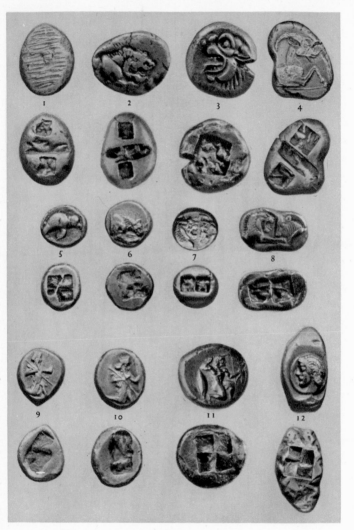

Early gold and silver coins of Lydia, Ionia and Persia, *c.* 700–500 B.C.

Early silver of Aegina, Argos, Paros, Corinth, and Athens, c. 660–530 B.C.

Early silver of Acanthus and tribes of Thrace and Macedon, c. 550–520 B.C.

3

Silver of Athens: (32) under Peisistratus, *c.* 566 B.C.; (33) under Hippias, *c.* 516 B.C. 0.8 and 1 in.

4

34

Silver of Peparethus: Grapes, winged god, *c.* 500 B.C. 1.1 in.

Silver of Greek States in South Italy: *c.* 530–510 B.C.

6

Early silver of Greek cities in Sicily: *c.* 520–490 B.C.

7

47a

Athens: Ten-drachma coin struck *c.* 486 B.C., from surplus silver in the state-owned mines. 1.4 in.

8

47b

Athens: Reverse of same ten-drachma coin, c. 486 B.C., showing the owl of Marathon. 1.4 in.

Silver of Olympia: (48) Eagle and thunderbolt, *c.* 520 B.C.; (49) Eagle and Nike, *c.* 480 B.C. 0.8 and 0.9 in.

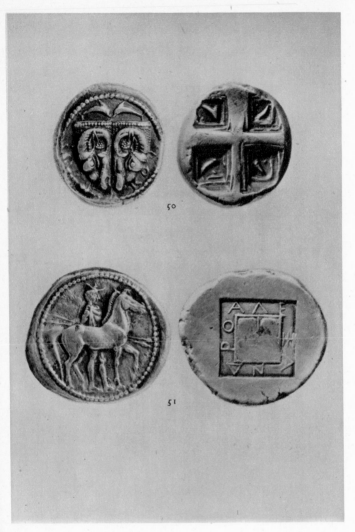

Silver: Delphi (50), rams-head drinking cups; *c.* 478 B.C.; Alexander I (51),
Horseman, *c.* 479 B.C. 1.1 and 1.3 in.

11

52a

Syracuse: Ten-drachma coin with chariot; struck 479 B.C. commemorating victory over Carthage. 1.5 in.

52b

Syracuse: Reverse of same ten-drachma coin; 479 B.C.; Goddess with resemblance to Queen Demarete. 1.5 in.

Silver: Cnidus (53), Lion, Aphrodite; *c.* 470 B.C. Lycia (54), Aphrodite, Syn-symbol; *c.* 475 B.C. 0.7 and 0.8 in.

14

55

Silver of Aenus: Hermes, Goat and primitive idol on throne; *c.* 470 B.C. 1 in.

56

Silver of Aetna by the Aetna Master: Seilenos, Zeus on throne; 470 B.C. 1.1 in.

16

57

Silver of Catana by the Aetna Master: River-bull, Nike; 461 B.C. 1 in.

17

58a

Silver of Naxos by the Aetna Master: Head of Dionysos; 461 B.C. 1.2 in.

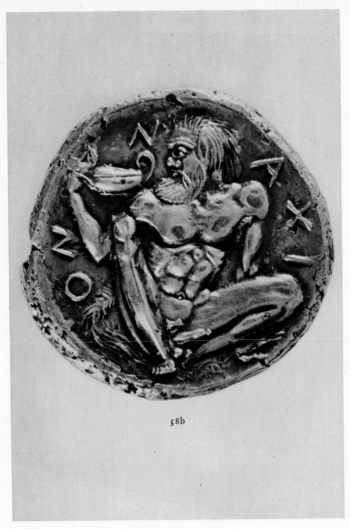

58b

Reverse of same coin by the Aetna Master: Seilenos with cup; 461 B.C. 1.2 in.

Silver: Selinus (59) divine chariot; (60) Herakles. Reverses river-gods; both *c.*
465 B.C. 1.1 and 0.9 in.

61

62

Silver coins with chariots: Catana (61) Apollo. Gela (62) river-god. Both *c.* 450
B.C. 1.1 and 1.1 in.

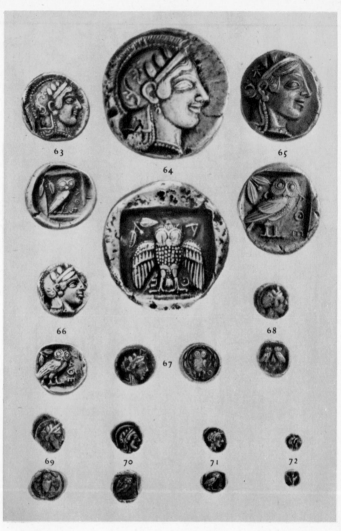

Silver: ten denominations current in Athens during the fifth century B.C.

22

Silver 'Athene' coins struck in South Italy c. 445–410 B.C.

23

Silver: Olympia (80), Eagle. Nike; 448 B.C. Troizen (81), Athene, Trident; *c.* 460 B.C. 0.9 and 0.7 in.

82

83

Corinthian silver: Pegasus. Athene. Corinth (82), *c.* 450 B.C.; Ambracia (83) *c.*
440 B.C. 0.8 and 0.8 in.

84

85

Syracusan silver: Both, Chariot and Goddess's head. (84) *c.* 455 B.C.; (85) *c.*
445 B.C. 1 and 1.1 in.

Silver by Euainetos: Chariots and divine heads; both *c.* 425 B.C. (86) Syracuse;
(87) Catana. 1 and 1.1 in.

88

Silver of Catana by Herakleidas: Apollo, Chariot; c. 415 B.C. 1.1 in.

28

89

Silver of Syracuse by Eukleidas: Chariot, Helmeted goddess; 412 B.C. 1.1 in.

29

90a

Silver of Syracuse by Kimon: Head of Arethusa; *c.* 408 B.C. 1.2 in.

90b

Reverse of same coin by Kimon: Chariot and Nike; *c.* 408 B.C. 1.2 in.

91a

Silver of Akragas engraved by Myron: Chariot of Helios; *c.* 408 B.C. 1.5 in.

91b

Reverse of same coin engraved by Polykrates: Eagles on hare; *c.* 408 B.C. 1.5 in.

92

93

Silver: Terina (92), Nike and Nike; *c.* 425 B.C. Croton (93), Herakles and Apollo; *c.* 430 B.C. 0.8 and 0.9 in.

Silver: Metapontum (94), Goddess, Barley; *c.* 410 B.C. Gold: Syracuse (95), Goddess, Herakles; *c.* 395 B.C. 0.8 and 0.6 in.

96a

Silver of Syracuse by Euainetos: Head of Arethusa; *c.* 395 B.C. 2 in.

96b

Silver of Syracuse by Euainetos: Chariot and arms; *c.* 395 B.C. 2 in.

97

98

Silver of Olympia: (97) Zeus, Thunderbolt; *c.* 420 B.C. Mende (98), Dionysos,
Vine; 430 B.C. 0.9 and 1.1 in.

Silver of Rhodes: (99) Helios, Rose; *c.* 408 B.C. Cyrene (100), Zeus, Plant;
c. 400 B.C. 0.9 and 1.1 in.

39

Silver of Sybrita: (101) Dionysos, Hermes; *c.* 360 B.C. Cydonia (102), Nymph,
Bitch; *c.* 360 B.C. 0.8 and 1 in.

Silver of Pheneus: (103) Maia, Hermes; *c.* 390 B.C. Megalopolis (104) Zeus, Pan; *c.* 370 B.C. 0.9 and 1 in.

105a

Silver of Clazomenae signed by Theodotos: Apollo; *c.* 370 B.C. 1 in.

105b

Clazomenae: same coin, reverse; Swan, wings open; *c.* 370 B.C. I in.

106

107

Silver: Olynthus (106) Apollo, Lyre; *c.* 360 B.C. Gold: Panticapaeum (107)
Seilenos, Griffin; *c.* 380 B.C. 1.1 and 0.7 in.

Silver of Olympia: (108) Zeus, Eagle; c. 340 B.C. Delphi (109) Demeter, Apollo;
c. 335 B.C. 1 and 1 in.

110

111

112

Silver: Massalia (110); *c.* 350 B.C. Gold: Metapontum (111), *c.* 334 B.C. Silver: Tarentum (112); *c.* 344 B.C. 0.8, 0.5 and 0.9 in.

Silver: Trapezus (113); c. 410 B.C. Sinope (114); c. 405 B.C. White gold: Cyzicus
(115); c. 350 B.C. 0.7, 0.8 and 0.8 in.

Silver: Alexander portraits. (116) mint Alexandria; contemporary 326 B.C. (117) issued by Lysimachus posthumously c. 300 B.C. 1 and 1.1 in.

48